I0519257

Cryptocurrency for Beginners

How to Take Advantage of the Biggest "Millionaire Maker" of the New Era, Including Bitcoin, Altcoins, and NFTs

Greg Middleton

© Copyright 2022 - All rights reserved.

The content contained within this book may not be reproduced, duplicated or transmitted without direct written permission from the author or the publisher.

Under no circumstances will any blame or legal responsibility be held against the publisher, or author, for any damages, reparation, or monetary loss due to the information contained within this book, either directly or indirectly.

Legal Notice:

This book is copyright protected. It is only for personal use. You cannot amend, distribute, sell, use, quote or paraphrase any part, or the content within this book, without the consent of the author or publisher.

Disclaimer Notice:

Please note the information contained within this document is for educational and entertainment purposes only. All effort has been executed to present accurate, up to date, reliable, complete information. No warranties of any kind are declared or implied. Readers acknowledge that the author is not engaged in the rendering of legal, financial, medical or professional advice. The content within this book has been derived from various sources. Please consult a licensed professional before attempting any techniques outlined in this book.

By reading this document, the reader agrees that under no circumstances is the author responsible for any losses, direct or indirect, that are incurred as a result of the use of the information contained within this document, including, but not limited to, errors, omissions, or inaccuracies.

Table of Contents

Introduction

Cryptocurrency is a form of money you will never really get to see, but it has turned many people into millionaires. It has been an item of debate ever since it came out, and despite many people having their doubts, cryptocurrency has survived through some of the toughest economic blows.

The world is ripe for a digital currency, and there is no denying the enormous potential crypto has worldwide. The problem is that you probably don't know much about crypto.

Sure, it gets discussed on TV and in the markets, yet it is not discussed at those times in detail. If you search the web, you will find many different articles, but it takes too much time to decipher all the information you need to know. You want to start trading, but to do that, you need to understand the foundation of cryptocurrency.

This book is designed for people starting from scratch. It isa starter kit. You do not need to have any prior financial knowledge, and you do not need to understand how blockchain works before coming here. This is a safe space for beginners, where technicalities get explained or simplified, and complicated concepts (such as blockchain) come with a flood of analogies to give you the necessary mental pictures.

Using both platform recommendations and explanations of online safety and trading tips, everything you need to start your trading journey is all here, including the tools to keep learning as cryptocurrency is still a new technology and even experts are still trying to figure it out.

Taking an unbiased viewpoint, you will also come to understand both the brighter and the darker sides of cryptocurrency, thus allowing you to make the logical choices necessary to improve your chances of success.

Your trading journey has just begun, so join me as we dive into the introduction of cryptocurrencies.

Chapter 1:

What You Need to Know

About Cryptocurrency

Cryptocurrency is a digital form of money. This means that you cannot ever hold a physical form of Bitcoin in your hands. The Bitcoin picture of a gold coin is purely an artistic design, when, in reality, Bitcoin is strings of code formed through the blockchain.

Sounds a whole lot like the "Matrix" movies, but let's move on.

There is a lot to unpack about cryptocurrency, starting with the digital currency itself and how it differs from the normal or fiat currencies we know and use on a daily basis.

Currencies

What exactly is a currency? It is a medium used in exchange for different products or services. It is money and normally has either been paper or metal coins. These kinds of currencies are issued by governments and are called fiat currencies.

These currencies have been used worldwide for at least 3,000 years.

But the difference nowadays is that modern money is practically worthless in and of itself. Paper does not have the same value as gold or silver, and the idea of paper money was first developed in China in 1000 BC. But it took a long time for the rest of the world to catch up.

According to WorldAtlas.com, there are officially 180 national forms of currencies in circulation, and 66 of these countries use the U.S. dollar or have pegged their currencies to the dollar.

There is no doubt that each currency has its own value. However, an Indian rupee does not have the same value as the British pound and nor does the Japanese yen have the same value as the South African rand. In order to change one form of currency to another, an exchange rate is needed to compare one currency to the value of the currency in another country.

Exchange rates are normally known as free-floating or fixed. Free-floating occurs when the exchange rate rises or falls in the foreign exchange market. An example of this are the fluctuations of the U.S. dollar. However, a currency can have its value pegged to another currency at a fixed change rate, such as the U.S. dollar. A good example would be the Hong Kong dollar, which has pegged its dollar to the U.S. dollar, and therefore the value differences are minimal.

Currencies are normally controlled by governments and financial institutions, which leads to the biggest differences between traditional fiat currencies and cryptocurrencies.

Crypto Introduction

As mentioned, crypto is a form of digital currency that runs on cryptography in order to stay secure and prevent counterfeiting. Most cryptocurrencies run on blockchain technology and are decentralized.

This means that cryptocurrency is not run or regulated by the government; rather, it is run on a distributed ledger (checking out blockchain and mining will help to explain just how cryptocurrency functions).

But cryptocurrencies' defining feature is their transparent nature as well as being, in theory, immune to any sort of manipulation or government interference.

You can either purchase cryptocurrencies on an exchange platform or mine them from their blockchain network.

Crypto History

So how did cryptocurrency come to be?

In the 1980s, the idea of a cryptocurrency started to take form. David Chaum invented digital cash that relied on cryptography in order to verify the transactions and keep them secured. However, only in the 1990s did the protocols for cryptographic software start to develop properly.

Then in 2008, Satoshi Nakamoto (a pseudonym as no one has yet proven who is the inventor of Bitcoin) published a paper, "Bitcoin: A Peer-to-Peer Electronic Cash System." This was the map for a system that would be a form of digital currency that does not require the interference of a third party.

Pros and Cons of Investing in Crypto

No system, digitally or currency is perfect. No investment is ideal, but some are safer and some offer greater rewards with bigger risks.

So we'll be diving headfirst into both the pros and the cons of cryptocurrency that really determine whether or not people are willing to deal with the drawbacks while hoping to receive the benefits.

Pros:

- A whole lot of personal information is secured when working with cryptocurrency. When you are signing up on different platforms for trading, or even your bank, there is a whole lot of personal information that you need to share. Even when you are offering someone your credit card for payment, you need to give them a PIN. However, how confident are you in the safety and the security of your PIN? But when it comes to crypto, you have two keys: the first is the public key that acts like a bank account number and the second key is your private key that you never have to share with everyone.

- The transfers of the transactions are far more secure and faster. How long does it take to make an international payment or receive an international payment? In my case, it can take up to four to eight days to receive an international transaction. But when it comes to cryptocurrency, it could take only a couple of minutes or even a couple of seconds. The transfers are also far safer and cannot be intercepted.

- Crypto also has a wide variety of anti-inflation properties, including the fact that there is a predetermined quality of coins for periods of time. For instance, Bitcoin has only 21 million coins that have been issued.

- Crypto is very volatile, which can be both an advantage and a disadvantage. Volatility means the rewards can be so much higher and greater. This means the amount of money you can earn with crypto can be literally in the millions.

Cons:

- Volatility is at the top of the list, despite the ability to turn many people into millionaires, it is just as possible to lose money. So as much as it has made some people's day, it has also robbed other people of their fortunes. It depends a whole lot on the skills, mistakes, and luck that occurs while people are making investments.

- Considering how young cryptocurrency is, it hasn't proven itself out in the long-term investment field. The currencies are widely known and have gone through incredible volatility, but their future is still not completely certain. Although there are many indications to show that cryptocurrencies are very likely to stay, that is still not completely confirmed.

- Cryptocurrencies have a large amount of scalability issues. Scaling is the ability for something to grow (with its revenue far outgrowing its expenses). Cryptocurrency is not built for use by too many people, as the more people who use a blockchain network, the slower the transactions go. Although it has not yet been a problem, the more people who will be adopting crypto can certainly make this a huge issue.

- Scammers and hackers love to target crypto users and crypto exchange platforms, particularly because of how untraceable these activities are. If you get scammed from your crypto, the chances of you retrieving your money are impossibly slim.

It is up to you to decide whether the rewards are worth the risks, and even if they are worth the risk, you need to be wise with your financial allocation. Cryptocurrency investments, due to their risky nature, should be the minority holding among your overall investments.

Blockchain for Beginners

Blockchain is the most difficult concept to understand as a whole. Luckily, unless you are planning on diving headfirst into mining, you only need to understand the basics of blockchain in order to work with it.

Blockchain is a public distributed ledger. This means that it records all the transactions while performing them, and it is known to be tamper-proof.

Blockchain Explained

The best way to explain blockchain is to break it up into a pictorial example. Imagine you want to buy a car. Every car comes with its own ledger to explain its history and to understand what money has been spent on it. You are looking at a Jeep and the owner has a transaction ledger that lists:

- 2015: Paid for a new oil filter

- 2017: Car service

- 2018: Dents fixed, paint touched up, windows Replaced

- 2019: Service, fan belt replaced

However, when you read the list, it states:

- 2015: Paid for a new oil filter

- 2017: Car service

- 2018: Aircon fixed

- 2019: Service, fan belt replaced

Can you tell what is wrong with these lists? It is evident that information has been changed, and the owner is obviously hiding indications that this vehicle has possibly been in an accident.

So, if you cannot trust the owner of the vehicle, how can you solve this problem of improper record-keeping? You get yourself a middle-man to keep all the records of the transaction. But guess what? Even middle-men are capable of making mistakes, offering bribes, and being biased and more.

In comes blockchain. Whenever a transaction is made related to the car, it is recorded as a block of information. The very first block of information is created (generally called the Genesis block), and it is set up digitally. When the first block is designed, a special key is created (a hash). If any information is changed on the blockchain, this completely transforms the design of the first key.

Then a second transaction is made and a second block of information is formed. But before the second key is designed, the first key has been placed into the second box. So if information changes in the first block, it changes the first key that, in turn, changes the second key.

What does this mean?

It means that, although the information can be changed in a blockchain, it makes tampering really obvious. Why?

Well, you now have a string of blockchain information, but there isn't just one copy. There are hundreds to thousands of copies of the blockchain all syncing over a certain period of time. If the blockchain doesn't match up with 51% of the other copies, then the information gets changed back to the original authentic information.

This is why cryptocurrency is known to be tamper-proof.

Analogies

Another good analogy is the glass box. Blockchain works a whole lot like walking into a bank filled with glass boxes. You can see everything going on inside of the boxes, but you cannot access the information inside them.

If you own cryptocurrency, you will have public and private keys. The public key acts like the address of the glass box, and the private key allows you to open the safebox. You do not own the safebox, but you can decide what happens with the contents.

Hashes

Hashes are what are often called the keys within the blockchain, and they are a critical element as to why blockchain works.

A hash allows you to enter a specific amount of information, which could be something as simple as the name of an essay about why crabs run sideways. The hash will encrypt this information and give a specific output number. For example, if you have a 1,000-word essay about crabs and you place it into a hash that outputs seven encrypted digits, you will receive this: 83-

0%hf. Then, if you place another hash, crab, then the encrypted digits you might receive are: j2b8ef5.

Regardless of the title of the information, you will always receive the same number of outputs.

Hashes are a core part of what makes blockchain work so well in keeping the information anonymous.

That is all well and good, but how exactly does blockchain information get verified and confirmed? What happens if someone tries to cheat the system? This is where crypto miners come into play.

Mining Summary for Beginners

Crypto mining is known to both verify and process the transactions taking place with a cryptocurrency. Miners are rewarded with tokens. Cryptocurrency miners have to work between proof of work (PoW) and proof of stake (PoS).

PoW and PoS

PoW has to verify a transaction, just as a miner's computer will have to solve complex mathematical puzzles. Bitcoin works on PoW, and so does Ethereum (however, Ethereum is currently working on switching to PoW).

PoW is known for using a heavy load of electricity, and there are many questions in regards to how ecologically friendly cryptocurrency is because of this system.

In contrast, PoS is used when miners stake their own tokens based on their motivation and leverage, so that they can make their own verification nodes. Other miners are then picked at random to verify a transaction. If they get the information wrong, however, they are at risk of losing their coins. But if their verification is correct, then they will receive a reward. The more cryptocurrency coins they stake, the greater their chances a miner will have to be chosen.

PoS is known for using significantly less computing electric energy. For this reason, many cryptocurrencies are built with PoS.

So now you should know about the different cryptocurrency tokens, after understanding their fundamentals.

Chapter 2:

What You Need to Know

About Different Coins

There are over 17,000 different cryptocurrencies in the world today, so you can imagine that there is a lot of competition. This also means that your choice of investments in tokens (different coins of crypto) will have to be very careful and wise.

The one tactic to make the best choices would be to find out about the different cryptocurrencies, their histories and their pros and cons. But for the sake of sanity and the impossibility of writing about 17,000 different crypto, when the information you are looking for is how to invest, perhaps it is best to equip you with some of the top cryptocurrencies and leave it up to you to decide which coins you want to work with.

Bitcoin

I would be surprised if you found a discussion about cryptocurrency without Bitcoin being mentioned at least once. Bitcoin is the first cryptocurrency, and all other crypto inventions are called altcoins for this reason.

Bitcoin was launched in 2009 by someone or a group using the pseudonym Satashi Nakamoto, whose primary goal was to build a financial system based on trust.

Every single transaction that has ever taken place on Bitcoin is recorded and can be found on the blockchain. For this reason, since its launch, its value has risen dramatically.

You can buy Bitcoin on different exchange platforms that allow people to buy, sell, and trade different cryptocurrencies, and Bitcoin is available on the majority of them, considering it42% of the total market cap.

History of Bitcoin

Bitcoin has been through many ups and downs, and perhaps understanding the true volatility of crypto and Bitcoin's history will give you a good mindset:

- January 3, 2009, Bitcoin's Genesis block was launched. The next transaction took place a week later. Bitcoin did not have any real monetary value at this time, and the majority of people were just trading Bitcoin for the fun of it.

- May, 22, 2010, a man paid 10,000 BTC (Bitcoin) for two Papa John's Pizzas. Imagine how that man must be feeling right now.

- In 2011, other networks and blockchain were being built. Considering that access to blockchain's code is open source, and so anyone can learn how to create blockchain, it is not surprising how many crypto coins have been made.

- In February 2011, Bitcoin reached a value of $1.

- In June 2011, it reached $31, but sank again.

- In April 2013, Bitcoin rose to $200.

- In November 2013 it reached over $1,000.

- In 2017, it ranged from $10,000 to $68,990.

- In January 2022, Bitcoin hit $46,657.53.

During this time, Bitcoin underwent both panic buying and selling, a fluctuation in miners (who play a role in how important cryptocurrency could be). Many people have believed that Bitcoin would not survive and even crash during the pandemic. Yet the opposite seems to have happened.

But considering that these fluctuations are still ongoing, unless some way is found to fix the volatility, it is unlikely to be accepted as a form of official currency by most governments.

Altcoins

All the other altcoins account for the rest of the market cap, with Ethereum taking up 19% of the total market cap. That leaves about 40% of the market cap to other altcoins. Tether, in third place within the marketplace, accounts for just 3%. It is important to note that the cryptocurrencies' total market cap is over a trillion dollars, so 3% is still a great amount of value.

What does this tell you? It should tell you, especially as a beginner, that it might be wise to work with the top cryptos until you have gained significant experience.

Ethereum

Ethereum is in second place, largely because it is a peer-to-peer network that can execute as well as verify a wide variety of networks and commands that are called smart contracts.

Ethereum is more than just a simple cryptocurrency. Its platform extends and offers a wide variety of services, including the possibility of creating your own crypto on Ethereum, having smart contracts executed, and being flexible in a wide variety of situations.

Ethereum's cryptocurrency is often called Ether, which you would be using when working on the platform, or when buying and selling NFTs (considering that 90% of NFTs transactions and creations are created on Ethereum).

Top Altcoins

Although they might not be in the top 10, some of the cryptocurrencies listed here hold a lot of potential and might be worth your time to consider:

- Lucky Block: Hosted by Binance's smart chain, Lucky Block has been lucky indeed with its growth and revolutionizing the overall lottery industry. With the level of transparency, time to make draws, and better chances of winning, you can imagine how popular the lottery could become.

- Aave: Considered by experts as one of the best cryptocurrencies working within the decentralized platform space, it even goes so far as to allow people to borrow and lend out their tokens with relative ease. With the use of smart contracts, interest rates and digital agreements can be set up. This means if you lend some money with this crypto, you can automatically gain interest and your money back over the specific time period due to this automated system. You don't have to go chasing after your money all across the globe or worry about accidentally forgetting about your monthly interest rate.

- Shiba Inu: This is another coin that has become popular on a meme, as it shares many similarities to Dogecoin, and it has gained a loyal community. But there are also tangible uses for this cryptocurrency that most other cryptocurrencies do not have at this time.

- Stellar (XLM): Along with a great platform, Stellar allows for a whole lot of fast payments with minimal fees. It improves the transaction services you will be receiving in comparison to the traditional banks.

- Cardano: This is one of the few cryptos that has been peer-reviewed by a variety of cryptocurrency experts, mathematicians, and engineers. It holds a lot of potential with its designs. However, it is still behind in comparison to Ethereum, and its development is slow. Thus, although the potential "Ethereum-killer," it still has a long journey ahead of it.

Reality of Altcoins

Altcoin's future is heavily dependent on Bitcoin. So if Bitcoin were to fail and crash, then the future of altcoins would remain equally uncertain.

As of May 2021, over 2,000 different cryptocurrencies have failed, and many more failures are going to occur as time moves on.

With so much demand out there, the world is still trying to catch up in crypto and still figuring out how to use crypto. It should be no surprise that the volatility and risk might not be worth your while until later.

The majority of investing experts recommend Bitcoin and Ethereum, and one should not necessarily dismiss some of the other top altcoins either.

Any new cryptocurrency, unless giving very clear and obvious indications (or you want to try it yourself because you enjoy risk), should be left alone for now. Stick to the top cryptos and what the majority of the market is working with.

Chapter 3:

What You Need to Know About Exchanges and Brokers

In order to purchase cryptocurrency tokens, you will need to buy them either through a cryptocurrency exchange platform or through a financial broker who specializes in crypto. These days, Bitcoin has become available in other official exchange platforms. However, most of the other cryptocurrency has yet to hit the official investment and exchange platforms.

Your choices of cryptocurrency exchange platforms are very important. This is because these platforms have become primary targets to cybercrime. So the security and the overall reputation of the platform are important.

Cryptocurrency Exchange Platforms 101

On a crypto exchange platform, the primary services would be the purchase and sale of crypto tokens. Different exchanges offer different kinds of services, such as the charts necessary to pick up on certain trends and speculate the price movements.

There are two primary forms of exchange platforms with crypto. One platform is a centralized exchange is the most popular form of a platform. It is, however, regulated by a specific organization. There are also decentralized exchange platforms that provide a high level of anonymity, but fewer people use it and it might not accept direct deposits from your card or banks (just crypto coins).

Exchange platforms are still new and developing, and there is a whole lot you will need to learn about them.

In order to invest on an exchange platform, you will have to open an account. Depending on the exchange platform, you will need to submit different amounts of information in order to qualify. Generally, the more information you need to submit, the more features an exchange provides (for example, having the ability to link your bank account or your cards to an exchange platform). Some platforms only want your verified email address and only accept crypto coins from your digital coins on your crypto platform.

Advantages of Centralized Platforms

- Centralized platforms are incredibly user-friendly. As a beginner, it might be wiser to use a platform you can understand. This allows you to view your account balances and make transactions through the application.

- These platforms are also more reliable by adding an extra layer of security and overall reliability when you are busy making the transactions.

Disadvantages of Centralized Platforms

- They are at a higher risk of hacking, as they are operated by companies and hold billions of dollars' worth of different cryptocurrencies, but specifically Bitcoin. One of the biggest examples would be that of Mt. Gox, which attempted a cybercrime theft leading to the loss of 850,000 Bitcoins and a suspension.

- Transaction fees are considerably higher in comparison to the normal peer-to-peer transactions. These platforms charge higher fees because of their convenience and services, and specifically with the very popular forms of cryptocurrency.

Advantages of Decentralized Platforms

- There is a decreased chance of being hacked as these exchanges do not transfer their money and assets through a third party.

- Market manipulation has decreased due to their nature, as users are protected from wash trading, and fake trading.

- There is a level of anonymity with decentralized exchanges, as they do not require you to fill up know-your-customer (KYC) forms and this allows higher levels of privacy for users in general.

Disadvantages of Decentralized Platforms

- They are a lot harder to work with as you must remember all your keys and passwords. If not, your assets will be lost forever and cannot be recovered. You will have to spend a whole lot of time getting to know the platform, unlike centralized platforms that offer the friendly user-interface process.

- You may struggle to find a decentralized currency that can trade fiat currencies for your digital ones, which means they are far less convenient for people to use unless they already own your cryptocurrencies.

- Considering that 99% of all transactions take place on centralized exchanges, you may have a tough time finding buyers and sellers for your cryptocurrencies. A low trading volume on a highly volatile coin can end up to be a very dangerous scenario overall (you are at a much higher risk of loss).

Top Centralized Exchanges to Consider

So which ones should you be browsing around for? Here are some of the top exchanges you can look at:

- Binance
- Coinbase
- Binance.US
- Kraken
- Bithumb
- Bitstamp
- KuCoin
- FTX
- bitFlyer

Top Decentralized Exchanges to Consider

If you like crypto for its anonymous nature, you should check out these decentralized exchanges:

- Uniswap
- Venus
- Tokenlon
- Sushiswap
- Compound
- BurgerSwap
- 1inch Exchange
- PancakeSwap

Everything You Need to Know About Crypto Brokers

This is where traders make use of brokers to buy and sell cryptocurrency on their behalf. According to the contract, investors don't actually own the crypto, as their money is safely stored in their broker's bank account.

Although they don't own the crypto coins, they will still be able to either profit from the fall or rise of the crypto price (depending on what strategy they have implemented). These derivatives are often called:

- Crypto CFDs: Allow traders to make speculations on the fall and rise of crypto prices. The traders can close the contract whenever they choose.

- Crypto Futures: Traders will enter a specific agreement with a broker to buy a cryptocurrency or to sell it at a specific price in the late future until the contract finally expires.

- Crypto Options: Works a whole lot like crypto futures with the obligations of buying and selling. However, there are certain options that allow traders to withdraw in the contract at the expense of losing one's deposit.

Pros and Cons of Crypto Brokers

Pros:

- Brokers have a higher level of security. Brokers are well-regulated and audited by reputable authorities.

- Brokers offer lower trading and withdrawal fees in comparison to exchanges.

- The liquidity of a broker is meant to keep prices quite high. Therefore, it would be easier to buy and sell cryptocurrencies on a broker's platform.

- You can make use of fiat currency and other cryptos to trade with your broker.

- The customer experience is also far better and more experienced in comparison to the exchanges. So if you have troubles with the platform, you might have better luck in comparison to crypto exchanges, as an overall beginner.

Cons:

- The market depth is limited as is the number of tokens. You will not be able to buy as many coins as you want.

- More experience is often needed when working with brokers, although the customer experience is better. Brokers are a little more advanced and a whole lot less user friendly. With the technicalities and the complexities, a lot more choices and strategies can be implemented. But this can only occur when you have a whole lot of experience.

Top Online Brokers to Use

- Etoro

- Gemini

- Stormgain

- BlockFi

- Localbitcoins

How to Choose a Crypto Broker Wisely

You want to look out for particular traits within the cryptocurrency brokers in order to best suit your needs and overall goals.

- You want to make sure the broker you choose has a solid financial backing. It means they need a large capital base (certainly has to be bigger than your own). This allows you to feel a great amount of security that the broker is not suddenly going to go bankrupt and crash, taking your money and crypto with it.

- You want to look for a cryptocurrency broker platform that works well and should be easy to use with a wide variety of advanced features. The platform should allow traders to manage the accounts quite easily and perform the whole technical analysis, and perhaps even have access to all the latest news from cryptos.

- You want cryptocurrency brokers to have a whole lot of confidence, experience, and reliability. The crypto market is new, but many of the brokers running the platforms do have a lot of experience in the market. You want to make sure the brokers running the platform have plenty of experience to increase your chances of success.

- You want to check out the commissions and the fees. You want to make sure the broker sets down the fees, and you understand what you are paying for. It is absolutely no use of you even establishing a proper budget of expenses when you do not know how much you are going to be charged for any sort of transactions.

So in conclusion, you want to find a reliable exchange/broker platform that can both aid you in your investments and strategies. The general rule of thumb would be that if you are trading with smaller amounts of money, then simply use an exchange platform, but when trading with larger amounts of money use a broker.

But how exactly do you go about trading and investing in cryptocurrency?

Chapter 4:

What You Need to Know

About Trading and

Investing for Beginners

Without a plan, you are planning to fail. Simple as that, and many people waltz into trading with the hopes of getting lucky enough. Although investing itself is quite a simple form and strategy, when you are trying to trade and focus on short-term trading, it will take a more strategic and overall complex approach in order to improve your chances of getting a profit out of it.

But imagine you walk into a field, and suddenly you have to play a professional world cup rugby game. You are expected to learn everything while on the field, while going up against professional traders who have been doing this for years. How do you think the game will go? Do you think you will win?

No? Why not?

And that is exactly why you shouldn't go into trading on the live crypto markets without practice first. People forget that when trading, you are actually competing against other people. Every win a person makes, someone else has a loss and vice versa. So when you want to compete against some of the top traders in the world you will need a good amount of practice.

Paper Trading

Paper trading is the way you can practice your different strategies and get yourself familiar with the live markets without actually risking any of your money in the first place.

Paper trading used to be people watching the live markets while writing down their trades on paper. They would keep track of their entrances and exits, as well as the profits and losses made during the fluctuations. It was all very grueling work, but luckily technology has changed a lot, making life a little easier.

Paper trading on cryptocurrency can now occur on simulations of the live market. You can make purchases, track your profits and losses, and see the supposed results of what would be occurring in your overall trade.

Paper trading on online platforms has increased the popularity of practicing trades, and some of the exchange platforms, as well as the broker platforms, allow paper trading. This means you can familiarize yourself with the different platforms and how they work without risking your money over a rookie mistake or misunderstanding.

Pros and Cons of Paper Trading

Pros:

- There is very little stress involved. Removing the emotional factor can allow you to approach trading in a logical and sensible manner. Having a clear head while practicing trading can help with the implementation of strategies, and seeing the results will allow you to grow your confidence, which leads to the second benefit.

- Whenever anyone tries something new, they can very well lack a good amount of confidence, which, in turn, can lead them to make a whole lot of mistakes based on fear. So having the confidence can allow you to spot the opportunities and learn to take the right risks.

- Practice, practice, and practice. There is a saying that practice makes perfect, and you can see that reality in any art, trade, or skill. You want to build your overall experience, and you want to understand what you are doing. You want to be able to identify patterns and understand how to apply a strategy. That all happens with practice.

- As for statistics, you can take your time building up the necessary statistics and knowledge over the crypto coins in order to design a great strategic approach.

Cons:

- Although it takes the emotional aspect away, it means you will have to learn how to deal with the emotional reality in the live markets. Just like practicing an instrument in your room is different than playing it on stage for over a thousand people, as you might get struck with stage fright. With trading, you might get struck with fear of missing out (FOMO), panic buying, and panic selling. The marketplace is rife with emotional traps, but the prices and fluctuations remain brutal in stone-cold logic. You want to dive head first into learning about trading psychology as you start trading in the live markets. Paper trading won't be able to teach you this.

- Paper trading does not take all the commissions and slippage fees into consideration. That means your calculations on your expenses and your profits are likely to differ somewhat. So it might be wise to tailor your expectations a little lower in order to not find yourself unnecessarily disappointed. Reality vs. fiction expectations do seem to creep in everywhere and that includes cryptocurrency. In fact, there is a much larger spread myth about crypto than the majority of other trading choices.

- Sometimes cryptocurrency paper trading fails to take into consideration how the global market can affect the crypto world. But time and again, whenever something happens within the economy, regardless of whether or not it is connected to crypto, something is bound to change within crypto. For example, as soon as the world started turning more digital with the rise of the Covid pandemic, people started to get more familiarized with cryptocurrency, and more attention was given to it. Now this is an overall positive impact, but there are negative blows against the crypto markets as well.

In conclusion about paper trading, there are far more pros that come with working on this platform than cons. The cons are fixed by you realizing that paper trading is not step-by-step accurate, and that you will have to take other factors into consideration when dealing with the overall live crypto market.

Understanding the Charts

But in order to implement a good strategy, you will have to learn to read charts. Candlestick charts are most commonly used in crypto, purely because of the amount of information you can get with a candlestick chart. It is better adapted for a more volatile investment format, and it allows you to identify the common trends occurring within the markets.

Crypto charts are graphical representations of the volumes, intervals, and price movements, and they are used to spot the different investment opportunities available.

It might be wise to look up a diagram of a candlestick chart and do your best to find the following:

- Dates
- Japanese candlesticks
- Price line of time that is remaining in a candle that is forming
- The open, the high, the close, and the low
- Trading pair
- Time frame
- Trading platform

A candlestick tends to indicate whether or not the price ended in a bearish pattern (when the price ended higher than when it started), and a bullish pattern (when the price ended lower than when it started).

When the price ends higher than the start price, the candlestick will be green. When the price ends lower than the start price, the candlestick will be red.

Support and Resistance

Understanding support and resistance is another one of the most important elements of reading a crypto chart. Support level is a reference to the price levels that an asset is believed unable to fall under over a specific period of time. It is normally represented by a line in the chart. Resistance levels are the point where the price is believed unable to rise across. This also comes in the form of a line. These support levels will help in making the overall decision on your market position on crypto (whether you should buy or sell).

Investment Strategies

One of the top recommended strategies for investing (especially long term) would be the dollar costing average (DCA). This is an investment strategy where you divide up the total amount you want to invest in a token and invest in it periodically.

So, for example, you have $1,000 you want to invest in Bitcoin. You divide it up into $100, and invest in Bitcoin on a Monday, at 2:00 p.m. every week. This helps to overcome the number of fluctuations that occur, and you will be able to buy more Bitcoin (or fractions of a Bitcoin) than if you had just invested all your money at once.

This is also a long-term strategy that is applied for various different stocks, bonds, and more. But it is particularly effective with more volatile assets as well.

Trading Strategies

Here are some day-trading crypto strategies that you should try out on paper trading and perhaps then on the live markets:

- Arbitrage crypto is when you purchase a crypto on one market and sell it on another exchange immediately for a higher price. This trick will require you to have a few different exchanges and a greater understanding of the price differences.

- Bot trading is when you make use of an automated trading tool to buy and sell at predetermined times and prices. These bots reduce the losses and risks when you work with them, and traders should certainly learn how to use them in order to stick to their goals when facing a trade.

- The long straddle involves putting a put and a call order, which means the trader is placing a bet on the crypto asset's price for the day. Where it will rise before they should exit with the bots or where they should fall and exit the market.

- Range trading involves pinpointing both the stable high and the low prices and identifying when the crypto asset is being oversold and when it is being overbought. When they identify this, they can either buy in as the price is getting lower (which will eventually stop and turn around because it was being oversold, or exit the market in time when it is being overbought).

Trading Tips

Here are some trading rules you should always follow:

- Always use a trading plan that rules when you are going to make an entrance, exit, and management for every purchase that you are going to make. Decide when you are going to exit with a profit or with a loss.

- Treat trading as if it were a business. Because unlike a hobby or a job as an employee, you have to put in a lot of time and commitment, and you are not always guaranteed results.

- Protect your trading capital as far as you can.

- Learn and become a student of the markets. You are never going to stop learning about trading, and you are going to constantly have to learn about the evolving markets. With crypto, it will be a lifelong process.

- Only risk the money in your trades that you can afford. The whole point of trading is to improve your monetary life, not to leave you worse off. But people have been borrowing money, dipping into their retirement fund, or placing money that had other purposes into crypto, only to come back empty handed and in greater trouble due to the financial loss.

- Develop a strategy and methodology based upon the facts you come across. Granted, it is not easy and takes time, but having a trading plan is worth it along the way.

- Always make use of a stop-loss and know when you should stop a trade.

Trading is not easy, and the reality will hit you hard once you reach the live markets. But playing it smart can reduce you a lot of pain and misery and increase your overall chances of success.

Chapter 5:

What You Need to Know About Online Security, Mistakes, and Scams in the Cyberworld

I am afraid most people do not take online security seriously until a cybercrime is committed against them. But by then, it is too late, and extensive damage has been caused. When you are delving into a world where people are especially targeted, you can see why a whole chapter needs to be dedicated to keep yourself safe online.

Although you don't have to become an ethical hacker yourself or have a law degree in cybersecurity, there are certain steps you can take to significantly boost your chances in not getting robbed blind online.

Just because you don't see a threat, doesn't mean it is not there.

Online Scams to Avoid

So what do you do to avoid the most common online scams? There are a few factors you need to understand. Scams will target everyone. So don't think you will be the exception to this. It doesn't matter your background, age, or income level. Everyone is going to be exposed or vulnerable to a scam at some point and time. Scams really succeed by looking very close to the real thing. Scammers are starting to get smart with technology and faking websites. They focus hard on building believable stories.

So how do you go about protecting yourself?

- Be always alert and aware that a number of facts do exist. You might be contacted by people with no initiative from your side. It can be via phone, email, text messages, or a social network site, so you need to be aware of the high probability of a scam. This can also occur with dating sites, so if you find people contacting you on those sites and talking about finances and on cryptocurrency, you can be assured that they are likely scammers looking for money, not love.

- Do not open any suspicious kinds of links, texts, emails, or attachments to any sorts of emails. You need to simply delete them as quickly as possible.

- Understand who you are dealing with. If you meet someone on an online platform of business, do a little bit of research. Do a Google image search as well as scour the internet to find people who have had dealings with them before. Even if an email or a message is sent from a friend that seems a little off or unusual, consider contacting your friend directly to check out if they sent it.

- Do not ever respond to calls where people are asking for remote access. Hang up immediately. It does not matter if they claim to come from a well-known and reputable company. People can claim to be pretty much anything these days, and that is how scammers get the best access to your computer. They will be promising to fix your computer or install for you a free upgrade, but they will be planting a virus, ransomware, or worse.

- Remember to keep your mobile devices as well as your computer secure. A whole lot of people may have an antivirus on their computer. They will, however, not think twice about their cellular device, which is perhaps just as vulnerable to hacks and viruses if not more so than their laptop. Remember that people also pretty much do everything on their phone. So all your information is readily available when people want to steal a whole load of money from you.

- Be very careful about any kind of unusual payment requests. Scammers love to ask you for unusual payment methods such as gift cards, checks, and certainly cryptocurrency as well. Considering crypto payments are irreversible, they are ideal for a scammer.

- Understand that scammers will either be claiming a problem or a reward. They love to use two tactics. Problems such as threats, viruses, or issues with your accounts are often used as a contact point, and they also love to instill a sense of urgency. But remember that professional companies and individuals will give you the necessary time to respond, regardless of whether or not it is a crisis.

Common Crypto Scams

Here are the four most common form of crypto scams that you may find:

- Imposter websites: Many scammers and hackers love to make websites that look almost identical to the authentic sites. And you might even be following the tip from a legitimate person. However, simply typing in the wrong link can cause you to enter the wrong page. So be sure to check out the HTTP and the HTTPS (the "S" in the HTTPS means that the website is secure). So any formal cryptocurrency website will be secured. The biggest giveaway when it comes to a fake and real website will be the URL. So always check it out before clicking on it. Clicking on the wrong link is like opening a door wide open for virus and malware. And sometimes it might even fool you into typing in the information of your public and private keys of crypto. Then you can kiss all your cryptocurrencies goodbye, because scammers are very quick.

- Many different cryptocurrency exchanges and platforms often offer their services on mobile apps. But that does mean that many scammers will be making fake apps that look identical or authentic enough to be a trading platform. Although fake apps are often reported very quickly, they still can attract unfortunate users and scam them before reporting occurs. Android users are more susceptible to the scams than iPhone users, simply because of the stringent security rules of Apple stores.

- Bad tweets, as well as a wide variety of social media trends and updates, can be the cause of many people falling into crypto traps. Make sure those you are following are not fake accounts and do not simply buy into everything that is taught on the platform. Fake news spreads all too easily and quickly online, especially within the crypto communities. It could make a certain coin appear all too important. Rather, anything you read on social media should be verified by a reputable source first.

- And scammers love to use emails, and they may contact you on behalf of a certain crypto company. Again, do not simply follow any kinds of links and information provided by emails. Rather, visit the authentic page yourself and contact the numbers and emails provided on the website and not on those provided by the emails.

Boosting Online Security

How can you boost your overall online security?

- Install a proper antivirus and keep it as updated as possible.

- Explore and find out as much as you can about the security tools. The more you know about your security, the better you can use it in the long run.

- Use a unique and original password for each and every account.

- Get a paid VPN and make use of it.

- Be sure to install a two-factor authentication for every software and platform that offers it.

- Make use of certain passcodes, even if they are only meant to be optional.

- Make use of different email addresses for all your various different accounts. This can allow you greater social security.

- Be sure to clear the cache. There are many different cookies that track your every movement. So clearing the cookies can wipe the various many different trackers away.

- Turn off all features that allow your password to be saved in browsers, and rather leave it for expert software whose very goal is designed to protect your passwords and keep them safe.

Avoiding Common Mistakes on Crypto

But sometimes scammers are not the cause of people's loss of crypto and money. Rather, it could be common mistakes made that cause such a wide variety of losses. Mistakes are normal for everyone, but it is best to avoid them where possible. So why not learn from the traders who have made these mistakes before you and save yourself a whole lot of time and effort?

First of all, many people start trading without a goal. But having no goal is having no direction, and if you are trading just because everyone else is doing it, you may be finding yourself pulling out the short end of the stick. The goals in the mind are the first steps to succeeding in crypto.

Despite crypto's volatile nature, you must not approach crypto with a short-term vision. Succeeding in crypto means abandoning the quick-rich philosophy and following through on the long-term goals. Rather consider earning smaller profits regularly over a long period of time rather than risking it all for a greater reward in the short term. You might just get lucky enough to receive such a great reward. But the loss can cause you to get kicked out of the game before you barely even started.

Another common mistake is jumping directly into trading and not trying your hand out first in cryptocurrency paper trading.

Another very common mistake is not having a solid trading plan when starting out. Unless you are planning on investing long term, which mainly involves keeping your crypto coins in a cold wallet and monitoring the markets over extended periods of time, you need to approach the market with a whole lot more strategy. Taking your chances on luck alone will cause you greater loss, much like people in casinos. Trading without a strategy is very similar to gambling after all.

Finally, many people make the mistake of not using a trustworthy cryptocurrency exchange platform. Security, reliability, and trust aspects go very much unnoticed, and people need to make extra sure that they are working with the right platforms in mind.

A common mistake would be a typo, forgetting your wallet in the car, and miscalculating the steps when walking down stairs and getting a small shock. But mistakes in the trading world will cost you a whole lot more, and they can knock you out of the trading world effectively. So be very careful with the choices you make. Quick impulse decisions should not be made unless all strategy and logic points to them.

Chapter 6:

What You Need to Know

About Digital Tools

Remember, trading works a whole lot like a game. You are competing against other traders. People need to be focused on picking up the trend first, exiting and entering the markets where they need to be, and staying ahead of the race. The best way to do that is to use all the latest tools dedicated to your success.

Tools to Track Your Trade

First of all, you want to check out trading platforms with trading charts. For example, Coinigy is one of the most widely used and popular tools within the market. Starting in 2014, they have always been growing, and can support 45 different exchanges, provide charts, and focus on quality support. This gives any investor a solid overall advantage.

Then there is Tradedash, known to support Bittrex and Binance platforms, as one of the biggest exchanges on the market. Tradedash is also a desktop application, which means extra privacy is added.

Charting Tools

How exactly are the charting tools going to help you? Charting tools really allow you to visualize the market. Having these trading indicators can help you identify the trends in order to get ahead in the market and incorporate your strategies. There are both paid and free versions:

Tradingview is a huge company that offers live charts for cryptocurrency and normal stocks. The majority of savvy traders make use of Tradingview as their main charting tool for crypto.

Market Data

Why is market data important? It allows platforms to offer real-time information that is both accurate in regards to the circulating supply, price action, total supply, and far more. With accurate data, you will have the necessary tools to make the best-informed decisions. Some of the best tools for this would be:

- Coinmarketcap is the site most used in the checking of price, supply, and volume of coins. They have quite a robust API, and it is helpful for everyone else to know just what the market can see.

- OnchainFX, much like its Coinmarketcap counterpart, offers a wide variety of unique statistics, as well as see the coins categorized as top losers, top gainers, scams and predictions.

Hard Forks, Airdrops, Block Halving, Others

Articles are not altogether the most reliable sources of information when it comes to crypto, as a lot is built on speculation. However, you want to make use of calendars in order to view upcoming events in the crypto world to help you best prepare accordingly.

There are tools such as:

- CoinMarketCal, which shows you all the different and upcoming events in regards to different coins.

- Coindar, which is focused on a sleek interface and reminds you of major events when they are going to happen soon.

Research Reports

Research reports are normally long, high-value documents that can give you fundamental analysis, technical analysis, and prior expert opinions on the markets in the past, in the future, and in the present.

A good one to check out would be the Crypto Research Report, which sends an in-depth quarterly report. It is also free for you to sign up and use it.

Trading Bots

Artificial intelligence (AI) is your best friend when you cannot spread your time and attention to everything. Working with trading bots can allow you to set up a wide variety of certain parameters and allow the bots to trade on your behalf. Good examples of good bots are:

- Haasonline has worked for over five years and has hundreds of technical indicators to choose from and is user-friendly.

- Gekko is a free open-source trading bot that can easily follow instructions and can be used on an overall wide range of exchanges.

Top-Quality Digital Wallets

You cannot trade without an electronic wallet, and it is best to go for a reliable wallet for best protection of hackers. After all, the quickest way to lose money is to have it stolen.

Some of the top wallets are:

- Metamask

- Mycelium

- MEW

- Exodus

You want to check out whether or not the trading platforms are compatible with your wallet and hopefully with your bank as well.

There are many other tools for you to take a look at and explore. You want to choose the tools that best suit your goals, and perhaps complete areas that you might be struggling in. For example, if you have difficulty picking up trends, then a charting tool will certainly come into handy.

Chapter 7:

What You Need to Know

About the Future of NFTs

Non-fungible tokens (NFTs) emerged shortly after cryptocurrency in 2014. But they have only become a viral phenomenon quite recently. If you find yourself struggling at the idea of trading, but have a more artistic/entrepreneurial side, then you should consider giving NFTs a go. NFTs have quickly become a multi-millionaire market, and there is no denying the potential NFTs also happen to hold in the future.

What Are NFTs?

NFTs are non-fungible tokens that are items that are continuously unique and absolutely cannot be replaced.

An example of a fungible token would be Bitcoin itself. You can swap one Bitcoin for another. The same can be said for a dollar note. You can swap one note for another. They are both the same, they can both buy you the same thing, and they are an exact copy.

However, non-fungible means that no value is the same. I suppose much like a fingerprint only if that fingerprint had a monetary value to it. Or it could be like a one-of-a-kind trading card.

NFTs can literally be any form of digital file. It can be a digital artwork, or a recording of you playing the guitar. Yes, it can even be a tweet you sent seven years ago when you might have been testing out twitter. After all, the first tweet was sold for a couple million dollars.

How Exactly Does an NFT Work?

On very technical terms, NFT is a part of Ethereum's blockchain. Ethereum, as you very well know, is a cryptocurrency like Cardano or Bitcoin.

But Ethereum's blockchain is known to support NFTs, and is one of the reasons why Ethereum has become so popular.

NFTs are a token, much like the Ether and the Bitcoin, but each coin is completely unique with different coding and value. Whenever you turn your digital file into an NFT, the process is called minting.

However, Ethereum is not the only blockchain shown to be compatible with NFTs, and some of the blockchains are being designed to be compatible, cheaper, and user-friendly to NFTs.

What Can You Do with NFTs?

You can sell them, keep them, invest them, trade them, and rent them. NFTs are very popular within the art world. In fact, many people consider they are the next step to art collecting within the digital world.

To give a realistic example, think about the Mona Lisa painted by Leonardo Da Vinci. There are thousands of copies all over the web and in books of the painting. But there is only one original painting. If the Mona Lisa were for sale, naturally the cost would be very high. You therefore cannot try and sell a copy of the Mona Lisa for the same price.

NFTs are the authentic and original files of artworks and can be sold as such. However, there is still a whole lot of controversy surrounding it, and many people are not convinced of purchasing such items for thousands of dollars for an item you can just copy and paste for free online.

But NFTs are technically giving you ownership of work. Only one person can truly own the original.

History of NFTs

But where did NFTs exactly come from? The very first NFT was created by Kevin McCoy, on May 3, 2014. He had a digital artwork called the "Quantum" minted, and this was way before the crypto market had become even remotely popular. In fact, cryptocurrency itself was still trying to walk onto the stage.

"Quantum," however, is now for sale for the price of $7 million, as it is the one-of-a-kind art piece that was first created within the NFT artworld.

As you may have guessed. McCoy was brilliant, and he and his wife had established themselves as first-rate digital artists, and there is no denying they were ahead of the game in this aspect.

But who can create NFTs now? Basically anyone. You can be an artist, an entrepreneur, the advocate of art, authors, social media personalities, celebrities, and so much more. You won't even need any extensive experience, but just be able to prove the NFT you have designed is indeed your very own content.

Anyone can also purchase an NFT and gain the rights to having the unique token. During this time, the future of NFT is still quite a little rocky, considering it is not even yet a decade old.

But what has happened since 2014–2022?

- 2012–2013: Colored Coins started to emerge just when the idea of NFTs started coming to light and were meant to represent real-world assets. Owning the asset on blockchain could very well be used to prove ownership of any asset. It could be from bonds, to plane tickets, to even real estate. Although it is a simple idea, mapping it out into reality is sophisticated.

- I think it's tragic how often systems get overly complex simply because of the corruption that resides within the economy. Crypto's whole goal was built on the distrust people had with the centralized banks and companies, as well as the payments being made on someone's behalf.

- 2014: Counterparty was launched and allowed as an asset creation inherent protocol that had been designed on the blockchain of Bitcoin. This would allow assets to be created on an exchange that was decentralized and provided a method for people to be able to create their own forms of crypto.

- 2015: Spells of Genesis was launched by game creators who were designing assets within the game and blockchain you could purchase, and they even introduced their very own currency inside of the game called BitCrystals.

- 2016: Trading Cards also started launching Force of Will cards on the Counterparty Platform and ranked fourth among card games in North America (purely because of the number of sales).

- 2016: Rare Pepe was designed on Counterparty, and memes started to take flight within the NFTs platforms. People even started adding certain assets to a meme that had been called "Rare Pepes." If you do not remember Rare Pepes, it was the funny/squiggly drawn frog face meme that had become an internet sensation.

- 2017: The cryptopunks came up, and NFTs really started to flourish. There were over 10,00 completely unique cryptopunks made, and they are now highly valuable.

- 2017: The CryptoKitties game started and allowed players to both adopt, breed, and take part in trading different cats. Each cat is unique and an NFT of its own, and the company and game became viral.

- 2018–2021: The NFT world truly exploded and moved into the mainstream. There is no true indication of what had suddenly caused this shift, but the transition really reached its highest point when Kevin Abosch partnered with GIFTO to sell crypto art for $1 million in a charitable auction.

A lot of people are conflicted about NFTs, with some saying they will fail while others see a very bright future for this exciting medium. What many people speculate is that NFTs are here to stay, but the future NFT is going to look radically different than it is today. As technology extends and keeps shifting towards the digital world, NFTs are likely to rise to prominence by playing a role in our everyday lives.

Pros and Cons of NFTs

So what are the advantages and drawbacks when working with this non-fungible token?

Pros:

- It is possible for anyone to invest into an NFT as it is accessible to everyone who has an internet connection. It is far easier to own a digital file, too, where it is tokenized by an NFT and can be sent to anyone anywhere in the world.

- NTFs are owned and secured within the blockchain. Considering blockchain's tamper-proof nature, you will not have to worry about proving your ownership of an asset, which allows the ownership to become far more transparent.

- If you are an artist selling your NFT, you can set up smart contracts to pay you royalties whenever someone else sells your artwork. Thus, the more popular your artwork becomes, the more passive income you will be receiving in the long run.

- You will also have greater opportunities to diversify your portfolio and learn more about blockchain.

Cons:

- NFTs generate a whole lot of electricity whenever there is a transaction made on them. It means that this excessive use of energy is contributing to the carbon emission that is overall not very eco-friendly. Artists who tend to use NFTs majority of the time are now focusing on pursuing more eco-friendly avenues for this technology.

- The majority of NFT sales will be taking place on the platform of Ethereum, and therefore might require you to purchase Ethers first before working with them. Investors who would want to purchase NFTs simply with U.S. dollars may have very limited options.

- NFTs are still incredibly new and volatile. So a lot of the hype around NFTs also consist of misinformation. Once cryptocurrency works on smoothing its own volatility, so will the same be for NFTs. But for now, you should consider investing in NFTs at the same risk as cryptocurrency.

How to Make Money Off NFTs

But how can you make money with NFTs? What are the steps you can go about to start benefiting within this digital world? Well, much like anything else, you start with learning how to make NFTs, what platforms and strategies you can undertake, and the cost and tricks to buying an NFT.

Minting NFTs

First, you will need to connect your crypto wallet to the NFT marketplace. For this example, I will be using OpenSea, one of the most popular platforms in the cryptocurrency market, that claims to have one of the largest NFT marketplaces.

Depending on the wallet you have, such as Coinbase or Metamask, you may be required to connect the wallet with the use of a QR code on your smartphone. Once your wallet is connected and your profile of the market is designed, you will need to complete your profile.

This works like any other artist's platform. You will tell a little about yourself, insert the links you may have about your website and social media pages, and be very specific about the form of cryptos you will be accepting when someone wants to purchase your NFT.

Then you will want to create your first item. On the Open Sea platform, you will find the button "create" on the homepage of the marketplace in the upper right corner. Then you will have to upload your digital file as a type in an NFT name. Make it catchy and memorable so that people who may consider buying your art can easily find it again. Again, having a portfolio of your work and a website can add to your credibility as a seller on this site.

You can also set up royalties for later on this site.

Also, make sure you have funds in your wallet. In order to sell an NFT, there are some networks and transactions taking place, and these transactions are oftentimes called gas fees. Once you have completed your first sale, you will want to have purchased some Ether or crypto that you can use and have in your wallet. You really need to choose the crypto token that the NFT market tends to prefer.

However, some marketplaces like OpenSea allow you to make direct purchases of crypto in your marketplace profile. You can then have your credit card connected, which will buy the necessary crypto and have it transferred to OpenSea.

Once you have created your NFT and have set up your wallet, it is time to list it for sale. This is where you can click on the "sell" button that is within the upper right corner on your description page of your NFT.

You will then have to work out the specific details in your sale. It can be a fixed price of crypto of your choice, and you can choose to have it done within a time auction. This means that people will be bidding for your NFT for a specific period of time. The highest bidder when the time ends will be the one purchasing your NFT. Once you have set up the complete payment system, you can click on the complete listing. Then you will be charged for a marketplace listing fee.

The fees will unfortunately vary from time to time, depending on when you upload and the current price fluctuations occurring within cryptocurrency. So you can never have a guaranteed fee price when it comes to cryptocurrency.

Once you have your NFT listed and for sale, it will be time to mingle with the customers. You can create many more NFTs, turn them into collections, which, in turn, might attract the art speculators or collectors. Depending on your marketplace, you could even transfer it to a different marketplace if you believe it will do better there.

Remember to bear in mind NFTs are very much still in their early days. To give an example, since the rise of cellular devices, it has started out quite simple. But now, the majority of people cannot do anything or access anything without their cellular device in hand. The smartphones are designed for everyday use.

NFTs are very much still in the "brick" phone phase, so as you are working with NFTs, keep a steady eye on all the updates and changes and adapt your investment strategy accordingly.

Platforms to Use

So what are the top marketplaces around for NFTs? Considering there are so many that sprung up so quickly, there are bound to be a couple of golden eggs mixed with some bad ones.

OpenSea

As used in the examples above, OpenSea is like Bitcoin on crypto. It is the leader in the NFT sales, allowing for a wide range of digital assets to be sold on its platform. You can sign up for completely free and go exploring on the offerings it has. It is known to be supportive of artists and creators, as well as a very user-friendly process in the design of your very own NFT. It goes so far as to support about 150 various different payment tokens in the world, and as you are a beginner in NFT, OpenSea is a really good place to start your journey.

Axie Marketplace

This is the marketplace you can shop for the video game called Axie Infinity. Axies are all about the mythical creatures that you can both buy, train, and compete against other players, earning rewards while doing so. You can also own lands on the Axies game and various other items that are used within the game. This platform is built on the Ethereum blockchain, and considering the multi-billion-dollar gaming industry, Axies have a whole lot of potential.

Crypto Punks/Larva Labs

This platform is best known for the CryptoPunks project, which was originally given away for free in 2017. However, some cryptopunks have now been sold for a couple million dollars. Larva Labs have been behind countless other art projects such as Auto Glyphs, etc. It has an amazing built-in marketplace and many other projects to keep tabs online.

Rarible

This is another huge marketplace for all different kinds of NFTs such as in OpenSea. It has art, music, and collectibles that can either be bought, sold, or created on the platform. You can buy and sell on this marketplace, but you will have to use its own token called Rari. It is also built on Ethereum's blockchain and has been partnering with some huge companies such as Adobe, Yum! Brands, and others.

Foundation

This is a very simple, easy design marketplace platform to sell digital art. It has sold over $100 million in NFTs and buyers simply need to have a crypto wallet with Ether in order to start making purchases.

Mintable

This is backed by the well-known billionaire Mark Cuban, whose goal is to have an open marketplace similar to that of OpenSea. In order to take part in the buying and selling of NFTs, you will need Ethereum on this platform, and it supports creators of all types.

Theta Drop

This platform is used for both video and TB on the internet. It launched with its debut of the World Poker Tour digital collectables and makes use of the platform in order to best stream the content.

Top Tips When Choosing Your Marketplace

NFTs marketplaces are the space you are going to be using in your investing of digital assets, arts, and collectibles, but there are a lot of choices out there. You want to choose one that suits your goals best, as well as the form of cryptocurrency that you would like to use in order to make transactions.

It is a highly speculative market, and certain NFTs may shoot for the stars while others remain stagnant in value. Considering the value is subjective and really determined by the overall uniqueness and reputation of the person who had made it.

Strategies to Use

So how do you go about selling NFTs? As much as we all wish it was as easy as listing on the marketplace and letting luck take its course, the marketplace does not work this way. Unless you have a well-established online media presence, it won't be as easy as everyone likes to describe it to be.

In fact, my biggest frustration when it comes to financial advice is the amount of work, time, and effort that is all left out when explaining a person's journey to making a good load of money.

Unlike trading, where the majority of your money making relies on your skill, strategies and luck, when it comes to NFT, you need a platform. So here is how to create yourself a social network platform in order to get the best results in selling your NFT:

- Find out about your target audience, the NFT community, and pay a lot of attention to where their platforms are. You want to start building a relationship with them and creating content that they actually happen to like.

- Do your online research to find, collect, and analyze the different demographics working on NFT. There are plenty of free resources out there for you to find the necessary data. All you need to do is dig as deeply as possible and take whatever valuable information is provided.

- Test out your approach and see the results. You can even create a demo version and test it on real people to see what their assumptions are and how they behave towards your posts. You can even consider sending a survey, asking people various forms of interview questions. This may cost you some money, but you will have some of the best results.

- Develop for yourself a good growth strategy that is based on the users and followers. Check out the competition of other people who are selling NFTs, and what their social media pages are looking like. Check out their engagement rates and create a growth strategy.

  o Start off small and slowly expand your base/page. Remember that even Facebook itself started small, and they used all the information they needed from what was available within their high school yearbook. Now it has become one of the most popular social media networks to this day. Have the same approach when approaching social media, and marketing your NFTs to people. Start small, grow bigger.

- Focus on one social media page at a time. Most people want to storm in and reach all NFT users on all platforms. But this will stretch you out too thinly, take all your time and so much more. So focus on building up one platform till it reaches a certain mark before moving on to the next one. Learn everything you can about that social media platform and apply it in your content.

Purchasing NFTs

If you want to purchase and invest in NFT, there are a few things you also need to look out for in order to make the best purchases with the most potential. Naturally, your goal would be to buy NFTs that will eventually grow in value over an extended period of time.

Unique Properties with the NFT

The majority of NFTs do come in collections, such as in the Mekaverse, Yacht Club, or even the Peaceful Groupies. Each collection has a variety of different properties, and the more properties they have, the higher value they should have. But at certain times, they don't.

Simpler avatars in the NFT world have shown to be of greater value, such as the basic Bored Ape NFT. So if you want to boost your chances of buying an NFT whose value is going to grow, check out the rarity within the properties that your NFT you are interested in happens to have. You also want to check the properties on the NFT to make sure it is authentic, as there are a lot of scam accounts uploading the copies of the popular NFTS. But they cannot replicate the properties, so always keep an eye out on this section.

You do want to check out the seller verification. Many platforms such as on OpenSea happen to have a blue verification tick on the accounts to show that the account owner can be trusted and are not trying to impersonate the accounts. So if you are looking for a well-known seller, be sure to check if the account has a verification tick.

Market Transaction Fees

Do not make or buy anything on the platform until you understand what the transaction fee is going to be or an estimate of it. OpenSea, for instance, charges around 2.5% of the transaction fee for the sellers. Buyers don't have to pay this transaction fee.

This is how the majority of other platforms happen to work, including Axie and the Known Origin.

Market Volume and NFT Liquidity

NFts do not have the same level of liquidity as the crypto coins, which is important to keep in mind. Selling an NFT may not be as easy or as quick as you could with a crypto, which can cause you to run into problems if you are investing into NFTs for a profit. So consider fractionalizing your NFT (splitting the collections) to boost their liquidity rates.

Check Out the Performance of Price on Other NFTs of the Seller

You want to check and confirm if you have made a good investment by checking out the seller's account. You can take a look at some of the previous sales they have made and the prices they are selling at. The more popular they are, naturally, the better and higher their overall prices will be. This means once you buy and resell their work, it might just turn out into a great potential profit.

Overall, NFTs are great investment opportunities, but it is always recommended to be playing it safe. You can make a huge profit or you can make a huge mistake. It is no surprise that cybercriminals are also frequently targeting the NFT industry in different ways. So always double check before making a purchase and be confident in the product that you are buying.

Chapter 8:

What You Need to Know About the Future of NFTs and Crypto

The future is exciting as it is uncertain. It is thrilling as it is scary. There is no denying that cryptocurrency and NFTs both are playing a huge role in the history of the world today, tomorrow, and who knows how long in the future.

Many people had come to believe in crypto's demise when it first came out. And every time Bitcoin seems to be at the mercy of the market, it has always found a way around. However, there are a few factors that are going to influence the direction of crypto, and what choices you are going to have to make. Environmental Impact of NFTs and Crypto

A lot of controversy has arisen about NFTs and crypto, but particularly NFTs. It is known that individual pieces of art have played a partial role in the carbon emission that has been heating up the planet. Certain artists do believe it is a problem that can easily be solved, while others face tons of backlash for launching their artwork on the NFT platform.

Digital artist Mike Winkelmann, who also goes by the pseudonym of Beeple, believes in the power of sustainable NFTs for the future. He sold a work for about $69 million and invested a certain amount of his profits into renewable energy, conservation projects as well as technology dedicated to sucking the dangerous CO_2 out of our atmosphere. A whole lot of other artists are following through on the same strategy.

Because NFTS are so new, the data that has been provided has not altogether been reviewed by a variety of outside experts. Therefore, people's analysis of the NFT market is considered one-sided.

And other artists have been asking the communities to leave the NFT alone, and instead to focus on the bigger companies that create far greater carbon emission than NFT is ever likely going to achieve.

The majority of this electricity consumption comes from the software roof of Work (POW) that acts as the security and verification system of crypto. Cryptocurrency miners have, as such, received just as much criticism over the power it takes to run the computers to mine one's crypto.

So when you are buying and selling NFT with the use of Ethereum, there is a certain amount of responsibility they hold to generating the emissions. Just how much emissions a person is talking about is entirely unknown. NFTs really make up a minor part of all the transactions being performed on Ethereum.

Figuring out the culpability that NFTs have is like trying to figure out how much your share of emissions was after a commercial plane flight.

But that doesn't mean NFTS are lost for good, as Ethereum is slowly switching over to Proof of Stake (POS). This means that the majority of NFTs artists can have the peace of mind that electricity consumption can literally drop overnight to almost zero.

But Ethereum is taking a while to adopt this change, and Ethereum will have to keep this promise otherwise its system will collapse.

Future of Crypto

So what do the experts overall believe crypto has in store? There is an estimate that the crypto market is going to be more than triple the valuation and investors, businesses, and brands will not be able to keep ignoring the rising power of crypto for much longer.

Cryptocurrency has pulled a whole lot of paradoxes, both of escape and falls everywhere, and investors strongly believe in regulation, yet are so concerned about what regulation can bring about.

The power of crypto largely relies on the power of public opinion. The number of investors in crypto have been steadily growing and seem to have exploded. More investors are evolving and adapting to the crypto market. Cryptocurrency is transforming from a hobby into a serious asset.

Half of all crypto users would be comfortable in adding crypto to ecommerce and even the older generations have started using crypto at much faster rates than expected. That means it is not just the younger generation working on figuring things out.

Investors also see the wide variety of benefits that crypto holds, but they equally have as many concerns about the drawbacks.

Recently, cryptocurrency has started to attract the traditional finance and institutions, who are busy storming to help cater to a growing demand, and with a large pool of investment and greater potential for the average person, it also threatens the digital currencies' ability to be able to operate outside of traditional finance.

Cryptocurrency has really started to rattle the power structure that has been contained within the market. The goal of crypto was to allow people access to the market and have ways to move money as well as make payments to goods and services, regardless of the circumstances of the individual. It removes the needs for traditional banks, as all you need would be an internet connection.

You don't even need to have an address to trade with crypto.

But now the future of crypto is different. People are neither so enthusiastic about mining bitcoin nor are they the only ones who have been profiting from their overall success. With the large amounts of power as well as electricity required, it can be difficult for independent users to be able to get involved.

Simultaneously, large corporations managed to cause the price of Bitcoin to jump in value at about 20% all within a single day. This makes a person wonder how immune the market truly is to manipulation.

Cryptocurrency has also caught the attention of the government, and the governments are now turning around with regulations or making it illegal. And many investors are actually welcoming these regulations so that not just anyone can make crypto.

But this goes against the initial goal of crypto, and this has become a point of concern for many investors.

As you can see, there is a constant push and pull between what crypto is, and how people want to work with it. It is a decentralized unique financial asset, but you cannot ignore what the volatility has cost people in the market.

As long as these paradoxes continue, the future of crypto will remain uncertain. But a good idea would be to keep an eye out of Bitcoin and the direction that it is heading. This is because Bitcoin is the one and only original crypto, and when it goes up, other altcoins' value goes up. When it goes down, other altcoins' value goes down. What happens to Bitcoin will have a major impact in the rest of the market after all.

Future of NFTs

There are several predictions about NFTs that you should consider as you start working within the cryptocurrency world.

- The democratization of art through the digitization of art has altered questions such as who the artists are and who can earn a living from art. Anyone with an internet connection has the ability to view artworks from a computer screen, and virtual reality has made it possible to view and visit galleries and museums on a digital level all within the comfort of your living room.

- There is an increased level of diversification and representations when it comes to displaying artists' work. Different people can come together to show the world their art and beauty, which is the goal of art isn't it? Giving worldviews and different experiences in comparison to one's own, allowing the perspective of the world to change.

- Art is going to look a whole lot different with NFTs and artists have better chances of actually getting paid for their work as well as the royalties when reselling occurs. It builds a fairer platform, where artists can deal with the buyers directly instead of a company that has the habit of ripping artists off of their money. You don't have to look very far to see where this is happening here and now. This will lead to increased freedom and independence for artists, who won't need to see the corporations feed their business instead.

- Art is not going to be the only aspect of NFTs. NFTs could also be designed into creating your own digital identity, proof of ownership over large assets, as well as play a role in the metaverse, where you can buy unique digital items to use within the boundaries of the digital world. The future of the digital world is a whole lot closer than most of us could ever dream.

Intro to Metaverse

Have you ever watched *Ready Player One*? This movie is perhaps the best representation of the metaverse, and what people are aspiring it to be.

The metaverse is defined as the expanse of digital space. People will be able to talk and interact with each other, as well as experience things like they can in the real world. And certainly buy things that you could not in the real world (like a dragon or a submarine).

First of all, what isn't the metaverse? Some people describe the metaverse as just another form of digital reality, but that isn't entirely true. The metaverse is not just limited to what the real world contains, but rather can operate on a different level.

It is also not just a theme park, as it has ideas and space similar to one. But the idea of just a digital theme park limits what the metaverse can offer. It can offer similar experiences, but again, extends it so much further than what you can imagine.

The metaverse may even be considered as a continuing realm of the real world.

I suppose gamers will have the best idea of the metaverse, as they have been exposed to such a wide variety of different worlds, features, and more. The metaverse is defined by a few different characteristics:

- The metaverse will be infinite. Just like the world wide web really has no limits, neither will the metaverse. It will not have any possible limit or end.

- The metaverse will be synchronous for users all over the world. This means, you will be able to safely interact with users all in real-time.

- The metaverse also has the ability to become a thriving economy, with so much to offer and receive similar experiences as to what you can manage within the real world.

- The Metaverse will also be interoperable. This means that people will be able to connect different parts together. So both huge companies and smaller groups can work on building the metaverse, and the world building does not fall into just one designer (this is perhaps, the one flaw of the movie Ready Player One).

Decentraland is one of the most well-known forms of metaverses that are currently existing today. It was launched in 2016, has a wide platform, and even big brands are starting to market there.

The entire community and world are built on the blockchain, and there is even a cryptocurrency being used to make payments for virtual items.

Decentraland has two primary tokens called Land and Mana. Mana is the cryptocurrency token, whereas the Land is the NFT representing the ownership of the real estate platforms.

Can you see where crypto and NFT are starting to play a role in the community already?

So now you can see, the metaverse already exists in part, and is likely to keep growing. You want to keep an eye on the prominent crypto and NFT being used there, as there is a lot of investment potential still waiting to arise.

Conclusion

Congratulations on making it to the end. There is a saying in a movie, an action-packed GI Joe film, when a character says "knowing is half the process." Although it was meant for missions within the movie, the quote itself could be applied in everyday life.

Knowing is truly half the journey, and the rest is up to applying it in action. So before you proceed any further, let's do a quick recap of everything you have learned within the book.

You have learned about cryptocurrency, its nature to be volatile, and the benefits and the cons of investing. You know that there is a wide variety of different tokens, but at the moment it is safer to stick with the top cryptocurrencies, especially as a beginner.

You also learned about the different exchange platforms in which to buy cryptocurrencies and the pros and cons of working on these platforms. You can choose between exchange platforms or brokers, depending on what best suits your needs and goals in the long run. Just be sure to pick your platforms wisely, as they are most often the targets of cybercrimes or could be scams themselves.

But along with the exchange platform, you will need to learn how to practice and incorporate different strategies to best boost your overall success. You can make use of paper trading and learn how to work candlestick charts and more.

Turning our attention away from cryptocurrencies, we then took a look at NFTs, where a person can both trade, sell, and invest in digital files. There is a lot of potential that NFTs hold, especially within the metaverse.

So it would be critically important to keep an eye on NFTs and cryptocurrencies within the metaverse world, as they are likely to become far more mainstream than they are even now.

So with the future so close yet so uncertain, all we can really do is watch and wait to see the directions that cryptocurrency and NFTs are heading towards. Everyone is talking about their potential and demise, and it is safe to say many people are equally divided about it. But considering crypto's rocky and new history, you cannot blame them.

There is no doubt that crypto can bring a whole lot of fortunes to the table, but people need to approach it carefully. Caution and risk need to be carefully balanced with an already risky investment choice. It has the benefits of reaping incredibly high rewards, but it can turn around with its losses as well.

So stay smart, stay safe, focus on the future, work in the present, and learn from the past to start your journey of crypto. May it be filled with great success and good fortune as you venture ahead into the incredible digital world.

References

Chen, J. (2020, January 31). *Exchange Rate Definition.*
Investopedia.
https://www.investopedia.com/terms/e/excha
ngerate.asp

Clark, M. (2021, March 3). *NFTs, explained: what they are,
and why they're suddenly worth millions.* The Verge;
The   Verge.
https://www.theverge.com/22310188/nft-
explainer-what-is-blockchain-crypto-art-faq

Currency History Definition. (n.d.). Investopedia. Retrieved
March   24,   2022,   from
https://www.investopedia.com/terms/forex/c
/currency-history-and-exchange-history.asp

Daly, L. (2021, September 24). *What Is Proof of Stake
(PoS) in Crypto?* The Motley Fool; The Motley
Fool.   https://www.fool.com/investing/stock-
market/market-
sectors/financials/cryptocurrency-
stocks/proof-of-
stake/#:~:text=One%20method%20many%20
cryptos%20use,add%20them%20to%20the%20
blockchain.

Editor1. (2021, November 12). *Pros and Cons of Investing In Cryptocurrency*. The World Financial Review. https://worldfinancialreview.com/pros-and-cons-of-investing-in-cryptocurrency/

Frankenfield, J. (2019). *What Is Currency?* Investopedia. https://www.investopedia.com/terms/c/currency.asp

How to read Crypto charts? (n.d.). Www.moneycontrol.com. Retrieved March 29, 2022, from https://www.moneycontrol.com/msite/wazirx-cryptocontrol-articles/how-to-read-crypto-charts/#:~:text=Crypto%20charts%20are%20graphical%20representations

Kaspersky. (2022a, February 9). *4 Common Cryptocurrency Scams and How to Avoid Them*. Www.kaspersky.com. https://www.kaspersky.com/resource-center/definitions/cryptocurrency-scams

Kaspersky. (2022b, February 9). *4 Common Cryptocurrency Scams and How to Avoid Them*. Www.kaspersky.com. https://www.kaspersky.com/resource-center/definitions/cryptocurrency-scams

Mediawire. (2022, February 4). *10 Best Altcoins to Invest in 2022*. The Economic Times; Economic Times. https://economictimes.indiatimes.com/industry

/banking/finance/10-best-altcoins-to-invest-in-2022/articleshow/89349596.cms?from=mdr

Portion. (2021, July 27). *The History of NFTs & How They Got Started.* Portion Blog. https://blog.portion.io/the-history-of-nfts-how-they-got-started/

Pros and Cons of Investing in NFTs. (n.d.). Investopedia. https://www.investopedia.com/pros-and-cons-of-investing-in-nfts-5220290

Rossolillo, N. (2021, December 9). *A Complete Guide to Minting NFTs (Using OpenSea as an Example).* The Motley Fool. https://www.fool.com/investing/stock-market/market-sectors/financials/non-fungible-tokens/nft-minting/

Team ZebPay. (2021, July 5). *5 common mistakes for a new crypto trader to avoid.* ZebPay | Buy Bitcoin & Crypto. https://zebpay.com/blog/5-common-mistakes-for-a-new-crypto-trader-to-avoid/

What Is A Currency War And How Does It Work? (2019). Investopedia. https://www.investopedia.com/articles/forex/042015/what-currency-war-how-does-it-work.asp

What is Blockchain Technology? - IBM Blockchain | IBM. (2022). Ibm.com. https://www.ibm.com/topics/what-is-

blockchain#:~:text=Blockchain%20defined%3
A%20Blockchain%20is%20a,patents%2C%20c
opyrights%2C%20branding).

What Is Ethereum? | AWS Blockchain. (2022). Amazon
Web Services, Inc.
https://aws.amazon.com/blockchain/what-is-
ethereum/#:~:text=Ethereum%20is%20a%20d
ecentralized%20blockchain,without%20a%20tr
usted%20central%20authority.

writer, F. B. F. T. A. F. is a, TheStreet, Edge, the editor
of H. R., trading, one of the first stock trading
websites H. is an expert in, Pittsburgh, technical
analysis with more than 25 years of experience
in the markets A. received his bachelor's in
psychology from the U. of, & Farley, is the
author of T. M. S. T. L. about our editorial
policies A. (2021, October 29). *Pros and Cons of
Paper Trading.* Investopedia.
https://www.investopedia.com/articles/active-
trading/072915/pros-and-cons-paper-
trading.asp

www.ingramcontent.com/pod-product-compliance
Lightning Source LLC
Chambersburg PA
CBHW071208120626
46546CB00006B/2469

* 9 7 8 1 9 5 9 0 8 1 4 7 0 *